Making A Difference

An old man came upon a little boy
at the sea shore
who was throwing starfish back into the water.
The man asked the boy
why he was wasting his time.
There were thousands of starfish
on the beach and he couldn't possibly
make a difference.
As he prepared to throw another starfish
the little boy replied,
"It makes a difference to this one."

Making a Difference

in
Physical Education

100 % Success and 100 % Participation

A Resource Guide for Teaching
Physical Education

by
John Thomson
1991 NASPE Elementary Teacher of the Year
Director of Educational Services
U.S. Games, Dallas, Texas

edited by
Nan Hazel
U.S. Games Educational Advisor
Physical Education Curriculum Specialist
Louisville, Kentucky

Published by UNEEDPE
Louisville, Kentucky

Making A Difference In Physical Education

ISBN: 1-892023-00-8

Author: John Thomson.
Editor: Nan Hazel.
Illustrator: Jennifer A. Iwasyszyn.

Printed by V.G. Reed & Sons, Inc.

Mission Statement

A hundred years
From now
It will not matter
What my bank account was,
The sort of house
I lived in,
Or the kind of car
I drove.

But the world may
Be a better place because
I made a difference
In the life
Of a child.

SPECIAL THANKS

Thank you to the many students I taught and to the teachers I worked with during my career for your many successful teaching ideas. Also, thank you to the many schools and organizations that hired me as a consultant allowing me the opportunity to develop and test my ideas.

Thank you, also to a special group of colleagues who contributed to my professional growth, who encouraged me to write this book and who collaborated with me over the years to create some of these teaching strategies: Cliff Carnes, Nan Hazel, Danette Lansing, Bob Parks, Roger Rodriguez, Anne Williamson and Bryon Yanke.

Contents

Preface

My intention in writing this book is to offer physical education teachers a detailed description of the physical education teaching strategies I have presented at workshops around the country. All of these activities have been used successfully with students to create an exciting and enjoyable learning experience. The activities focus on basic skills and are designed to accommodate various learning abilities. I have tried to provide a variety of strategies using supplies and equipment that motivate kids to learn, play and have fun.

This book is based on the the following characteristics of a quality physical education program:

- All students are participating at all time. Students are not standing in lines waiting to participate, e.g., relay races, skill practice.
- There are opportunities for different levels of success for all students rather than elimination-type activities.
- Traditional team sports are broken down into small group activities rather than team sports with one ball per class, e.g., kickball, softball.
- Time-limit challenges are used for activities rather than a set number of repetitions such as a set number of laps or push-ups.

Designing curriculum with 100% success and 100% participation is a real challenge. Here are some practices to consider when developing lessons/units.

- Plan for success the very first day. Repeat successes.
- Give simple rules.
- Correct one thing at a time.
- Move from strength to weakness.
- Learn from success, *not* mistakes.
- Maintain **high** expectations (No one rises to low expectations).
- Encourage students to:
  (1) Try their guts out!
  (2) Show BIG TIME manners.

- Provide Choices! Choices! Choices!
    Positive choices get positive results.
    Having a choice implies ownership.
    Taking ownership implies responsibility.
- Choices = Success = Participation.
- Remember:

TELL ME .... I forget
SHOW ME .... I remember
INVOLVE ME .... I understand

How To Use This Book

Overview

This book contains over 80 teaching strategies that will test and challenge all of your students. It is organized into eight sections. One section has physical fitness activities and seven sections are categorized by the supplies and equipment utilized in the specific activities in that section. The Sections are: Camouflage Fitness, Bean Bag and Ball Handling, Movement Cards™, Rubber Chicken Activities, Rubber Bass Activities, Spots and Cones, Cooperatives, and Specialty Activities. Each activity is organized in the following format:

- *Title:* The title gives an idea of what the activity involves. For example "Put and Take" requires students to *Put* a bean bag from the floor into the hand of their partner and then to *Take* it and place it on the floor.

- *Purpose:* All teaching strategies have an objective or purpose. We have tried to give you the primary purpose knowing that many of the activities will have many more purposes than listed.

- *Supplies:* Equipment needed for this teaching strategy is listed under this heading. Usually the amount of equipment will be given for one or two students or a small group. The number of students in a class will determine the total amount of equipment needed (See *Appendix A* for a *Recommended Physical Education Supplies* list to implement all the activities in this book for a class of 32 students).

- *Set-Up:* Tells you how students are grouped, their relationship to each other and the playing area. Keep in mind this information so that you will have 100% success and 100% participation, even though the activity can accommodate more students and less equipment.

- *Illustration*: Provides a graphic representation of students performing some phase of the activity. We hope "seeing is believing," and "a picture really *is* worth a 1,000 words."

- *Procedure*: Gives a brief description of what you want students to do. It describes the actual organization of the activity; the restrictions; some safety recommendations; the position of the students; and their relationship to other students, their space and equipment.

- *Variations:* Rather than create a totally new activity using a similar format, we provided some other ways to perform the skills identified, and to add some challenges for those students who are ready to move to the next level.

Grade Level Appropriate

During my presentations I have been asked about grade level appropriateness for activities. You will want to consider the overall goals and outcomes of **your program** and pre-skills of your students. Presenting new skills to students who do not have the necessary pre-skills to be successful will only frustrate them. While on the other hand, if your students are not challenged they may be bored. Either situation may cause discipline problems in your class. You are the best judge of appropriateness for your students.

For additional information regarding developmentally appropriate grade level activities, you may want to review the document *Moving into the Future: National Standards for Physical Education, A Guide to Content and Assessment.* This document identifies consensus statements related to what a student should know and be able to do by grade levels: k, 2, 4, 6, 8, 10, and 12. This document was developed and published in 1995 by The National Association for Sport and Physical Education (NASPE), and it contains input from hundreds of physical education professionals throughout the country.

Always remember:

Inch by inch, it's a cinch!
Yard by yard, it's too hard.

Safety

There is an element of safety that you will need to address in each individual activity depending on your class setting, number of students, student readiness, and equipment. Self-control, personal space and general safety need to be reinforced during each class.

Management Protocol

There are many times during your class when you want students to stop what they are doing, be silent, listen to you, or move to form a group. It's a lot of fun to have your own secret code for managing your class. Teach your students these *action words* and *phrases* to encourage them to LISTEN, then to THINK, then to MOVE.

When you say "Apples," students stand up.

When you say "Oranges," students sit down ."

When you say "Bananas," students scatter, in open space in the activity area.

When you say "Hawaii," this means break time, and students immediately relax on their back.

When you say "Huddle," students gather in front of you ready to listen.

When you say, "Are you ready?" students say all together "You bet!" Use this directive anytime you ask the students to perform a different task.

Camouflage Fitness

The following strategies are designed to improve physical fitness in a nontraditional way; therefore, the concept of *camouflage.* To insure success of all students these activities provide a time limit rather than a set number of repetitions. The use of time as the controlling factor instead of repetitions allows each student to progress at their own pace. To establish baseline data, individualized pretest of each activity is necessary, then each student will be able to set their own goals based on the principles of training. Begin by performing tasks for 10 to 15 seconds and increase time as endurance increases.

To encourage improvement, students need to identify each component of physical fitness related to each activity and to choose activities to improve their personal fitness. "For elementary school students, the emphasis is on awareness of fitness components and having fun while participating in health-enhancing activities that promote fitness. Middle school students gradually acquire a greater understanding of fitness components, how each is developed and maintained, and the importance of each in over-all fitness."*

All activities start and stop to music. A **Wireless Remote On/Off Switch** will save time and increase your effectiveness for using your tape/CD player, by allowing you to roam throughout the activity space. Simply plug the receiving unit into any standard 120V outlet and then plug the device you want to control by remote into it. The Wireless Remote works up to 50 feet away.

* National Association for Sport & Physical Education, *Moving Into the Future, National Physical Education Standards: A Guide to Content and Assessment* (St. Louis: Mosby, Inc. 1995).

Where Are You?

Purpose: To develop mental fitness, mind and body connection, body awareness and identification, quickness and flexibility, listening and following directions.

Supplies: None

Set-Up: Scattered in open space facing the teacher.

Procedure:

This activity is a mental warm-up for any lesson and a way to get students focused on listening.

Teacher asks the question: "Where are you?"

Students respond by flexing their biceps and saying, "Here I am."

Then students touch and say in rhythm:

"Head, shoulders, knees and toes, ankles, legs, heart and nose."

Repeat the sequence. Students respond with an accelerated rhythm.

Variation:

- Perform to audio tape: Campbell-Towell, Lee. "Where Are You?" *The Alligator Purse*, San Antonio: Cats Paws in Motion, 1994.

Hi Fives

Purpose: To improve cardiorespiratory fitness, and to review and master locomotive skills.

Supplies: Music.

Set-Up: Scattered in open space.

high five

high tens

low five

Procedure:

The teachers names a specific locomotor skill, (walk, run, skip, gallop, or slide, and a level, (high, medium, low). On a signal (music, bell or whistle), students move around the gym performing the movement. When the music stops, they see how many different students they can give a Hi-Five to and get a Hi Five from before the music starts again. Every time the music starts change the locomotive movement. Every time the music stops change the method of the Hi Five, e.g., behind-the-back, over-the-head, doubles.

Variations:

• Use movement sequences such as 4 walks high, 4 skips medium and 4 hops low, repeat.
• Let the students' creativity take over.

Four Side

Purpose: To increase physical fitness and and to review selected motor skills.

Supplies: Four blank cone-clip-on message signs, 4 open top cones, Vis-a-Vis® markers

Set-Up: Students on the perimeter of a rectangle activity area.

Procedure:

The teacher writes a different locomotor skill on each message sign board attached to an open-top cone and places one of them at each corner of the rectangle activity area. Examples: walk, jog, skip, hop, jump, gallop, slide, bear walk, crab walk, walk while doing arm circles, grapevine walk, seal walk, lame dog walk.

Facing counter clockwise, students find a space on the perimeter of the rectangle. When the music starts all students walk forward and perform the locomotor movement noted on the message sign. Change the movement at each corner.

Variations:

- Use all physical fitness components, such as running and skipping for cardiovascular endurance; and, crab, bear, and seal walk for upper body strength and endurance.

Vegas Hop

Purpose: Use as a cardiorespiratory warm-up, and to develop rhythm, motor skills, smooth transition of skills and directionality.

Supplies: Audio tape player and tape: Billy Joel. "All Shook Up," *Honeymoon in Vegas* (Music From The Original Motion Picture Soundtrack), Sony Music Entairnment Inc.,1992.

Set-Up: Students scattered in open space.

Procedure:

Traditional *Bunny Hop* moves to a non-traditional beat.

Students perform the following sequence to the beat of the music while moving throughout the activity area.
Heel-Toe R (right), Heel-Toe R, Heel-Toe L(left), Heel-Toe L,
Hop Forward, Hop backward, 3 Hops Forward
Repeat sequence.

On an oral command from the teacher, students move and hook up with a partner to make a *Vegas Hop* pair. Keep the beat while moving to connect with other groups. Eventually the whole class should be in one *Vegas Hop* line.

Tag Along

Purpose: To improve cardiorespiratory endurance, to follow the leader and to practice handling equipment.

Supplies: Any piece of equipment that does not bounce and that is easy to handle for every group of 4-6 students; e.g., deck ring, bean bag, relay baton.

Set-Up: Groups of 4-6 students in single file formation.

Procedure:

Students walk in single file with the leader choosing the path. The first student hands a deck ring, bean bag, etc., to the next student in line, and they hand it to the next student. When it reaches the last student, they jog to the front of the line and continues the hand off progression. Everyone is to keep moving during the hand-off and while the last student moves to the front of the line.

It is the responsibility of the group leader to maintain an appropriate speed for all team members.

Variations:

- Use a variety of equipment.
- Set a specific circuit/path to follow.

Steal the Bacon
Seated Position

Purpose: To develop listening and reaction time skills.

Supplies: One bean bag for every 2 students (try a heart squeesh or a frog bean bag).

Set-Up: Partners seated cross legged facing each other, scattered.

Procedure:

A bean bag is placed directly in the center between the partners. (If you have an odd number of students have them form a triangle and place the bean bag in the center). When the teacher calls out "ready," students place their hands on their thighs. When the teacher calls out "right," "left,"or "both," the students react quickly by reaching for the bean bag with their right hand, left hand or both hands before their partner. Repeat.

Variations:

• On the command "ready," student place their hands on their head then reach for the bean bag from that position. Use other ready positions such as placing. hands on the hips, eyes, or back.

• Change partners often.

Steal the Bacon
Push-Up Position

Purpose: To develop listening and reaction time skills, laterality, and upper body strength.

Supplies: One bean bag for every 2 students (try a heart squeesh or a frog bean bag).

Set-Up: Partners scattered throughout the activity space.

raised leg   raised leg

Procedure:

Partners face each other while in **THEIR** version of the "up" position of a push-up. A bean bag is placed directly in the center between the partners. (If there is an odd number of students form a triangle and place the bean bag in the center). When the teacher calls out "right" or "left," the students react quickly by reaching for the bean bag with their right hand or left hand before their partner. **Only** use the commands "right" or "left" or you may have some bloody noses. Repeat.

Variations:

• From the push-up position, have students hold their right or left leg up while waiting for the command to grab the bean bag.

• Change partners often.

Steal the Bacon
Sit-Up Position

Purpose: To develop listening and reaction time skills, abdominal strength, and laterality.

Supplies: One bean bag for every 3 students (try a heart squeesh or a frog bean bag).

Set-Up: Groups of 3 students scattered.

Procedure:

Two students are in the *down* position of the sit-up position facing each other with their knees bent, feet flat on the floor, with toes touching their partner's toes. The third student dangles the bean bag (bacon) in the air directly above the center of their feet. When the third student gives the command "right," "left," or "both," they *sit-up* to grab the bean bag. Positions rotate after a designated number of repetitions.

Variations:

- Partners perform "X" number of sit-ups before they grab the bean bag.
- This activity is also called *Quick Hands*.
- Change positions often.

Push-Up Hockey

Purpose: To improve reaction time, upper body strength and endurance, balance and body control.

Supplies: One bean bag for every 2 students.

Set-Up: Pairs scattered in open space.

Procedure:

Each partner is in **THEIR** version of the "up" position of a push up facing each other about 4 to 5 feet apart. One person has a bean bag and tries to **slide** it through their partners arms. Their partner **reacts** and **blocks** the bean bag from going through. Take turns. A point is scored each time the bean bag goes through their opponents goal (arms). No signal is given to start. Students must react to their partner's movement

Variations:
- Use groups of three or four students, and add more bean bags.
- Change the equipment by using a larger or smaller bean bag, fleece ball, or small foam ball.
- Move students closer together as they become quicker and stronger.

Push-Up Toss

Purpose: To improve upper body strength and endurance, balance body control, and eye-hand coordination.

Supplies: One bean bag for every 2 students.

Set-Up: Pairs scattered in open space.

Procedure:

Partners are in the "up" position of a push-up facing each other 4-5 feet apart. On a signal (music, bell or whistle) partners toss a bean bag--right hand to right hand. Partners see how many tosses they can perform in a set amount of time. (Perform task for 15 seconds and increase time as endurance increases.)

Variations:

- Toss beanbag left hand to left hand.
- Toss right to right then left to left, continuing the sequence.
- Hold one leg up and off the floor while performing the task.

Toss Up and Over

Purpose: To improve upper body strength and endurance, cardiorespiratory endurance, balance, body control and agility.

Supplies: One bean bag for every 2 students.

Set-Up: Pairs scattered.

Procedure:

One person is in the "up" position of a push-up. The other person stands behind their partner facing their partner's feet.On a signal, the student in the push-up position tosses the bean bag with their right hand up and over their right shoulder so that their partner can catch it. After catching the bean bag the receiver, using a sliding step moves to the left side and hands the bean bag back to their partner. The push-up student takes the bean bag with their left hand. The receiver slides back behind their partner ready to receive a left-handed toss. The receiver, after catching the toss, slides to the right of their partner who takes the bean bag with their right hand.

Continue the sequence to see how many successful catches a pair makes in a set time limit.

Put and Take

Purpose: To improve upper body strength and endurance, balance, sequencing and cooperation.

Supplies: Two bean bags for every two students.

Set-Up: Partners facing each other scattered in open space.

Procedure:

One student is in the "up" position of a push-up facing their partner. The seated student is in a cross legged position with their palms *up* at knee level. Two bean bags are placed on the floor directly in front of the student's hands in the push-up position. On a signal, the push up person picks up a bean bag with their right hand and PUTS it in the left hand of their partner; and then picks ups the other beanbag and PUTS it in their partner's right hand. When both bean bags are in their partner's hands, the push up person reverses the procedure and TAKES the bean bags from their partner's open hand and places them one at a time on the floor. Change places.

See how many times partners can do the sequence within a specific time.

Oil Well Push-Up

Purpose: To develop upper body strength and endurance, rhythm and cooperation; and, to review and master the overhead pass.

Supplies: Playground ball or any other ball suitable for an overhead pass. One ball for every two students.

Set-Up: Partners facing each other scattered in open space.

Procedure:

Partners kneel and face each other. One student holds the ball to make an overhead pass. The other student holds his hands up ready to receive the ball at chest height. The passer makes an overhead pass to his partner, moves his hands to the floor and then performs a modified push-up. He then instantly rises up to a kneeling position to receive the ball back from his partner. His partner passes the ball and then performs his push-up. Partners should mimic the up and down motion of an oil well. Perform as many oil well push-ups as you can in a set amount of time.

Variations:

- Partners move far enough apart to perform a bounce pass.
- When strength improves use a light weight (4-5 lb.) medicine ball.

Oil Well Sit-Up

Purpose: To develop abdominal strength and endurance, cooperation and rhythm, and to review and master overhead pass.

Supplies: One playground ball for every 2 students (or any other ball suitable for overhead pass).

Set-Up: Partners facing each other scattered in open space.

Procedure:

Partners face each other 5-6 feet apart, knees bent, feet flat on the floor. The student with the ball starts while on their back holding the ball over their head, arms straight. The student without the ball is sitting up waiting to receive the ball from their partner. When the music starts the student with the ball sits up and makes an overhead pass to their partner. Their partner, upon receiving the ball, moves to the down position holding the ball with their arms extending over their head. Repeat, performing as many oil well sit-ups as you can in a set amount of time.

Variations:

- With toes touching, partners hand a bean bag back and fourth to their partner while perform oil well sit-ups.
- When strength improves use a light weight (4-5 lbs.) medicine ball.

Pop-Up

Purpose: To improve overall fitness and agility and to master leaping skills.

Supplies: None.

Set-Up: Pairs scattered in open space.

Procedure:

One student lies flat on their stomach. Their partner stands at their waist, facing them. On the signal the person lying flat "pops-up" into a bridge (cat stretch) position. The student standing crawls or scrambles under and through their partner's bridge as quickly as possible. Once all the way through the bridge, they stand up and the bridge lies flat on their stomach again. This time their partner leaps over them.

Continue the sequence for a set time limit before partners change positions.

Overs

Purpose: To improve overall fitness and agility, and to master leaping skills.

Supplies: None

Set-Up: Students scattered in open space.

Procedure:

One half the class is in a modified crab position (legs straight). Upon a signal from the teacher (music, bell, whistle), the other half of the class counts how many different "crabs" they can run to and LEAP OVER within a set amount of time.

For safety purposes it is important that the crabs are spaced throughout the activity area and that they do not move.

Change places.

Variations:

- Use various methods of traveling e.g., skipping, galloping, sliding.

Unders

Purpose: To improve overall fitness and to develop agility.

Supplies: None.

Set-Up: Students scattered in open space.

Procedure:

One half the class is in the bridge (cat stretch) position. Upon a signal from the teacher the other half of the class, the "movers," count how many different "bridges" they can run to and crawl or scramble UNDER within a set amount of time. *It is important that the bridges are spaced throughout the activity area.* The "movers" must crawl under every "bridge" before they can repeat.

Change places.

Variations:

- The "movers" must use the bear walk or the crab walk position to go to the next bridge.

Flip-Flop

Purpose: To improve overall fitness and agility.

Supplies: None.

Set-Up: Students scattered in open space.

Procedure:
Make sure students can successfully perform *Overs* and *Unders* from the previous pages.

One half of the class is scattered throughout the activity area in either the "bridge" or modified "crab" position. The other half of the class, the "movers," travel under the "bridges" or over the "crabs." After a student goes under a bridge, the bridge FLIPS over into the modified crab position. And when a student goes over a crab, the crab FLOPS over into a bridge position.

In a set amount of time to how many bridges can students can go under and how many crabs they can go over. Movers should **alternate** going over a crab and then under a bridge.

Bean Bag
and
Ball Handling

This section focuses on activities that use various types of balls and bean bags to teach and practice manipulative skills such as catching, throwing, dribbling and passing. In order for **all** students to participate and for **all** students to be successful, it is necessary for **all** students to work individually and in small groups performing these skills with various weights, textures and sizes of balls, discs, bean bags, etc.

Selecting and caring for equipment is critical to providing a quality program for all students. Few teachers have an unlimited budget, or have the budget to purchase everything they need every year. Even though balls, ropes and other soft goods are considered consumables, teachers want their equipment and supplies to last longer than one year. Listed below are some hints for selecting and caring for your teaching supplies so that *maybe* they will last a little longer.

- Consider overall outcomes of your program and existing inventory before ordering anything new.
- Purchase institutional quality items. Discount store "specials" are usually constructed of material for home use.
- Over inflating balls is a major problem. If the seams on a ball look stretched, then it is over inflated.
- Playground balls are especially susceptible to over inflation. They bulge before they become firm. Therefore, a playground ball is "squeezable,"when fully inflated.
- Prevent a major cause of ball failure by providing lubrication to the ball value stem when inflating.
- Motivate students with old activities using innovative items, such as, frog bean bags, rubber chickens, rubber bass, wiggle jiggle balls, Gatorskin® Softi balls, etc.
- Select ball carts that hold different size balls.
- If there is a problem with any equipment, call the company.
- Economize, comparison shop.

Touch and Go Tag

Purpose: To review and master tossing and catching, chasing and fleeing, and to develop cardiorespiratory endurance.

Supplies: One bean bag for every 2 students.

Set-Up: Pairs scattered, facing each other at least 2 giant steps apart.

Procedure:

When the music starts, partners toss and catch a bean bag. When the music stops, the person with the bean bag tries to tag her partner. If the tagger tags her partner, she drops her bean bag. Her partner picks up the bean bag and becomes the new tagger. When the music starts again, partners get together and toss and catch with each other again.

Note: Start and stop the music often (10 to 15 seconds). Always tag with the free hand using light touches.

Variations:

- Must tag a teacher designated body part (elbow, shoulder).
- Each time the music starts, students must change the type of toss, e.g., backward, under leg, behind back.

Coconuts

Purpose: To improve fundamental motor skills and develop cardiorespiratory fitness.

Supplies: One hoop (coconut tree) and two coconuts (various equipment that will not roll, such as, spider ball, bean bag, flying disc.) per student.

Set-Up: Hoop scattered with 2 coconuts inside.

Procedure:

Each student stands beside their "coconut tree." When the music begins, students go to another coconut tree, gets a coconut and brings it back to their "tree." Only **ONE** coconut can be taken at a time, and students must return it to their "tree" before they can get another one. Students cannot guard their hoop nor can they take from the same hoop twice. See how many coconuts students can gather before the music stops.

Start and stop the activity often.

Variations:

• Travel between "trees" performing various locomotor skills.

Back Off

Purpose: To review and master different throwing and catching skills with different manipulatives.

Supplies: One Poly Spot™ or small boundary cone for each student, and one piece of equipment used for throwing and catching for every 2 students, e.g., flying disc, bean bag, football, rubber chicken, foxtail, deck tennis ring.

Set-Up: Partners facing each other with enough room to move backwards into open space.

Procedure:

Partners stand 2 giant steps apart from each other with a poly spot or cone directly in front of them as a location marker. The purpose is to successfully throw and catch an object to each other staying behind their marker. Each time the catcher successfully catches the thrown object, the **catcher** moves her marker back one step. If the thrown object is dropped or caught in front of the marker, the marker is moved toward the thrower one step. **Only the catcher's mark is moved.** Continue throwing and catching to see how far apart partners can get during a set time limit.

Change the throwing object every 2-4 minutes.

Foxtail® Math

Purpose: To practice throwing and catching skills.

Supplies: One Foxtail® Softie for every 2-3 students. (A Foxtail® Softie has an extra soft sponge ball sewn in place with nylon mesh, and a three color, 30" nylon tail attached to it.)

Set-Up: Pairs scattered in open space.

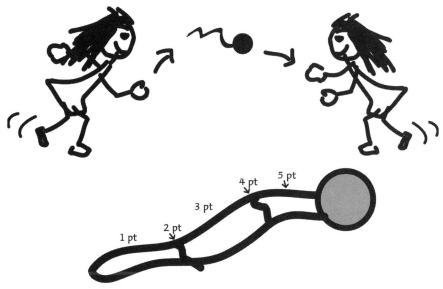

Procedure:

"All throws and catches must be made by the tail only."* Points are made depending on which color of the foxtail is caught. The hardest catch (scoring the most points) is the color closest to the ball.

Assign points to each color, e.g., the color closest to the ball is "5 points" the next color is "3" and the color on the end is "1." Students also score points for catching the tail between two colors. If the foxtail is caught between the first two colors, students score "4" points. If it is caught between the last two colors, they score "2" points. See how many points partners can accumulate in a set amount of time. Multiply catch numbers to practice multiplication. Or start with 100 points and see how many catches it takes to get to zero by substracting catch numbers.

*Editors of Klutz Press and Mike Gallaghan, *The Official Foxtail Book* (Palo Alto: Klutz Press, 1991) 5.

Foxtail® Ricochet

Purpose: To practice throwing, catching, and striking skills.

Supplies: One Foxtail® Softie for every 2 students.

Set-Up: Pairs scattered in open space.

hit straight up
with back of hand

catch with
opposite hand

Procedure:
The Foxtail Law usually disallows catching the ball.* In this particular activity it is O.K. to hit ball.The student with the foxtail tosses it by the tail to their partner. Instead of catching the foxtail by the tail, the catcher must hit the ball into the air with the **back** of one hand and **catch** it by the tail with the **other** hand--thus a Ricochet. The catcher throws the foxtail back to their partner who catches it in the same manner. Repeat. When students are successful, they are to move father apart, if they are unsuccessful, they move closer together.

Variations:
- Students must catch the Foxtail by the tail with the same hand used to hit it.

*Klutz Press, p. 21.

Bombs Away

Purpose: To improve the skill of throwing at a moving object.

Supplies: For every 4 students: one ball and 2 items that can be thrown e.g., bean bags, Gatorskin® Softie balls, various sizes of playground balls, foam balls, fleece balls, foam discs, flying discs, super soft footballs.

Set-Up: Groups of 4 students scattered.

Procedure:

In each group of 4, the students determine 2 "rollers" and 2 "throwers." Standing about 10-15 feet from each other the rollers roll a ball back and forth between themselves. The throwers face each other on **opposite** sides of the path of the rolled ball. The throwers try to hit the rolled ball. Partners rotate after a certain amount of time or number of throws. Change throwing objects frequently.

Variations:

- Change the level of difficulty by changing the size of the rolled ball.
- Rollers bounce a ball back and forth and the trowers try to hit the ball.after the first bounce.

Arach Attack

Purpose: To improve ball rolling skills and estimation of applying force.

Supplies: One Spider Ball™ for each student. One 9" Poly Spot™ for every 2 students.

Set-Up: Pairs scattered in open space.

Procedure:

The objective of this activity is to "lag" a spider ball as close as you can to a poly spot (target). Partners set up their own course by **placing** the spot within a reasonable range. Each person takes her turn and rolls her spider ball from a designated place toward the spot: seeing how close she can get to the spot. The partner coming closest to the target with her spider ball is the next one to place the spot.

Encourage students to move around the activity area using both long and short courses.

No Bump Bowling

Purpose: To improve ball rolling and estimation of applying force.

Supplies: One Spider Ball™ for each student and one bowling pin for every 2 students.

Set-up: Pairs scattered in open space.

Procedure:
Partners establish their own boundary lines. The bowling pin is the target. Partners bowl (roll) their spider ball toward the bowling pin. The object of the game is see which student comes the closest to the bowling pin **WITHOUT** knocking it over (no-bump). Award a point for the closest spider ball to the pin. Establish new boundaries and begin again.

Variations:
- Change the distance.
- Instead of bowling pins, draw a "bullseye" on the floor with different scores inside each ring.

Continuous Bowling

Purpose: To practice rolling a ball at a stationary target.

Supplies: One Spider Ball™, one small bowling pin, and one 9" Poly Spot™ for every 3 students.

Set-Up: Groups of 3 students establish a Bowling Lane in open space.

Procedure:

The bowler rolls the spider ball toward the bowling pin trying to knock it down. The bowler then runs down to set up the pin (if it was knocked down). The retriever retrieves the ball--the retriever DOES NOT pick up the pin. The retriever takes the ball back to the poly spot. The spider ball is placed on the spot. The old retriever now stands in line behind the spot. The student who was waiting, picks up the spider ball and becomes the new roller. This is a **CONTINUOUS** rotation.

Guard The Pin

Purpose: To practice foot dribblling ball control in a group activity.

Supplies: Spider Ball™balls for one-half of the class, bowling pins for the other half.

Set-Up: One-half of the class scattered with a bowling pin, the other half scattered with a Spider Ball.

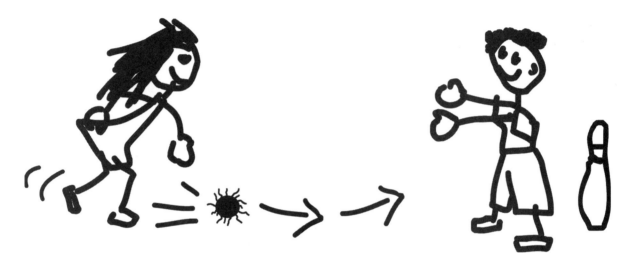

Procedure:

One-half of the class, the guards, is scattered throughout the activity area standing by (guarding) their upright bowling pin. Each student in the other half of the class has a spider ball. Upon a signal, they dribble their ball and try to knock down the bowling pins. It is the job of the "guards" to protect their pins. The guards cannot use their hands, they can only use their feet. The challenge is for the dribblers to knock down as many different pins as possible, in a set amount of time.

When a pin is knocked down the student sets it back up and continues protecting it. Positions rotate at the expiration of the time.

Variations:

• Allow only one dribbler at a time trying to knock down a pin.
• Partner students to work on passing skills.

Hoop It Up

Purpose: To improve eye-hand coordination, and to develop problem solving and cooperation.

Supplies: One hoop and one bean bag for every 3 students.

Set-Up: Groups of 3 students, scattered.

Procedure:

The person with the hoop stands between the other two students (the tosser and the catcher), who are facing each other. The distance is determined by the location and angle of the hoop. The object is to catch the bean bag after it has been tossed through the hoop. After every toss, the hoop holder changes the height, angle and/or location of the hoop.

Change the hoop holder often.

Variations:

- Use mathematics terminology to identify the angles of the hoop, e.g., parallel, perpendicular, right angle.

Basketball Tag

Purpose: To master passing and catching a basketball, and chasing and fleeing skills. To improve cardiorespiratory endurance.

Supplies: One basketball for every 2 students.

Set-Up: Pairs scattered, facing each other at least 2 giant steps apart.

Procedure:

When the music starts, partners pass and catch a basketball. The student with
the ball determines the types of basketball pass. When the music stops, the
person with the basketball is "it," and tries to tag his partner with his free hand.
If the tagger tags his partner, he hands the basketball to his partner. The student
with the ball then turns one complete circle: giving the chased student enough
time to move away. The student with the ball is now the chaser. When the music
starts again, partners get together passing and catching. Each time the music
starts, students must use a different type of pass.

Suggested passes: chest, bounce, overhead, baseball, right and left push.

Note: Start and stop the music often (5-10 seconds). Always tag with the **free
hand** using light touches.

The Shadow

Purpose: To practice basketball dribbling and pivoting skills.

Supplies: One basket ball or similar ball for each student.

Set-Up: Pairs scattered in open space.

follow leader

switch

about face

Procedure:
Partners each have a ball. One student stands behind the other in a line facing the same direction. Upon a signal (music, horn) both students start dribbling around the area in a follow-the-leader formation. When the teacher says "Switch," partners pivot and switch directions (about face). Partners switch the dribbling hand and follow the new leader. The teacher should say "switch" often and at random intervals. Students should never know when they are going switch: directions, hands, and leaders.

Variations:
- Students "switch" on a signal from the teacher such as a whistle or bell, after the students have mastered the technique of switching on a verbal cue.
- Use both basketball dribbling and soccer dribbling skills.

The Shadow Part 2

Purpose: To practice basketball dribbling skills.

Supplies: One basketball or similar ball for every student.

Set-Up: Pairs scattered in open space.

follow leader

rotate

Procedure:
Partners each have a ball. One person stands behind the other in a line facing the same direction. Upon a signal (music, horn) both start dribbling around in a follow-the-leader formation. When the teacher says "**rotate,**" the person in back moves up front to become the new leader. Students continue dribbling in the same direction while the new leader moves to the front. Following the new leader, both continue dribbling with the **opposite** hand. The teacher should say "switch" often and at random intervals. Students should never know when they are going rotate to the front:

Variations:
- Students "rotate" on a signal from the teacher such as a whistle or bell, after the students have mastered the technique of rotating on a verbal cue.
- Combine this activity with *The Shadow* (previous page). Students must be ready to "rotate" or "switch."

What's the Count

Purpose: To practice basketball dribbling and using sign language numbers.

Supplies: One basketball or similar ball for each student.

Set-Up: Students scattered in open space.

Procedure:

All students hand dribble freely throughout the activity area. When a student encounters another person both flash a **sign language number**, one through 10, with their non-dribbling hand. Students do not stop dribbling when a number is flashed--dribbling is constant. Each student tries to recognize and say the other person's flashed number. (See *Appendix* for *Sign Language Numbers.*)

Continue dribbling freely and encounter different students. Each time a new person is met, flash a new number.

Variations:
• Add, subtract or multiply the flashed numbers.

Knock-Out

Purpose: To improve basketball dribbling skills and body control.

Supplies: One basketball (or other similar ball) for each student.

Set-Up: Students scattered with a basketball in open space.

Procedure:
Upon the signal to begin, students dribble while protecting their ball and at the same time, trying to knock someone else's ball away from them. When a ball is knocked away, the student retrieves his ball and continues dribbling.

Variations:
- Establish a "Safety Zone," such as the basketball key. Students continue dribbling, even when they are in a safety zone. If there are students who stay in the safety zone too long, the teacher calls out, "change zones." This forces all students to leave a safety zone even if it is long enough to dribble to a different safety zone.

Tunnels

Purpose: To practice soccer dribbling skills (eye foot coordination).

Supplies: Enough balls for one-half of the class (any kind of ball comparable in size to a soccer ball).

Set-Up: One-half of the class scattered.

Procedure:
One-half of the students are scattered throughout the activity area. They are standing in tunnel position, legs spread wide apart. The other students, with a ball, are standing on the side lines. On a signal from the teacher, they foot dribble the ball through as many tunnels as possible in a set time limit. Dribblers cannot repeat a tunnel until they have been through all of them once.

Change positions.

Variations:
- Use hand dribbling skills.
- Warm-up for *Tunnels*--students dribble the ball back and forth through their partner's tunnel in a set time limit.

Close the Tunnels

Purpose: To practice soccer dribbling skills (eye foot coordination).

Supplies: Enough balls for 1/2 of the class (any kind of ball comparable in size to a soccer ball).

Set-Up: One-half of the class scattered, the other half with a ball on the side line.

Procedure:

One-half of the class is scattered throughout the activity area. They are standing in tunnel position, legs spread wide apart. The other students, with a ball, are standing on the side lines. On a signal from the teacher, they foot dribble the ball through as many tunnels as possible. After five soccer balls have gone through a tunnel, it is closed. A closed tunnel sits down with their legs crossed. Challenge the dribblers to see how fast they can *close the tunnels*. Dribblers cannot repeat a tunnel until they have been through all of them once.

Change positions.

Z-Ball™ World Records

Purpose: To improve eye-hand coordination, balance, quickness, and depth perception.

Supplies: One Z-Ball™ for every 3 students. A Z-Ball™ is a hard rubber, six-sided ball, approximately 2 1/2" diameter. The design allows it to pop, bounce and leap unpredictably in different directions.

Set-Up: Groups of three students scattered.

Procedure:

Students form a triangle at least 2 giant steps from each other, facing center. Groups need plenty of space as the Z-Ball take "wild" bounces. Students keep feet shoulder-width apart with knees slightly bent in the "ready position." he student with the Z-Ball tosses it up in the air so that it lands in the middle of the triangle. Do not toss the Z-Ball at any one person. Who ever is closest to the Z-Ball after it bounces once tries to catch it.

See how many times your group can catch the Z-Ball in a roll without missing. Set your own *One Bounce* **World Record.**

Variations:
- Allow the Z-Ball to bounce twice before it is caught.

Continuous Grounders

Purpose: To improve eye-hand coordination, balance, quickness, agility, and depth perception.

Supplies: One 9" Poly Spot™ and one Z-Ball™ for every three students. (A Z-Ball™ is a six-sided, hard rubber ball, approximately 2 1/2" in diameter. The design alows it to pop-up and bounce unpredictably in different directions.)

Set-Up: Groups of three students establish a pathway in open space.

Procedure:

The tosser stands on the poly spot. The catcher stands away from, and faces the tosser. The third student stands behind the tosser ready to take her turn.

The tosser throws a one-bounce grounder to the catcher. The tosser then runs down to become the next catcher. The catcher catches the z-ball and carries it back to the poly spot. The z-ball is **placed** on the spot. The old catcher now stands in line behind the spot. The student who was waiting, picks up the z-ball and becomes the new tosser. This is a **CONTINUOUS** rotation.

Quick Eyes

Purpose: To develop reaction time and visual tracking, and to master tossing and catching skills.

Supplies: One ball for every 2 students. Use balls of various size.

Set-Up: Pairs scattered in open space, one student with a ball..

Procedure:

The student with the ball is the tosser. The other student is the fielder. The fielder faces away from their partner. The tosser tosses the ball in the air directly **behind** the fielder's back. When the tosser says, "Go!" the fielder pivots, visually locates the ball, and catches it. Younger or less skilled students may let the ball bounce before catching it. The tosser should adjust the height of the toss to ensure the success of the fielder, with gradual increase of difficulty.

Variations:
- Vary the height of the toss
- Vary the size and type of tossed objects (e.g., bean bag, football, tennis ball).

Pop-Ups

Purpose: To develop reaction time, throwing and catching skills.

Supplies: One ball for every 2 students. Have balls of various size available.

Set-Up: Partners scattered in open space, one student with a ball.

Procedure:
One partner with the ball is the tosser, and the other partner is the fielder.
There are four levels of Difficulty.
Level 1--The fielder lies face down on the floor. The tosser stands facing the fielder about 6 feet away from the fielder's head. The tosser gives the command "Go," and tosses the ball **straight up into the air.** Do NOT toss the ball at the fielder; this will force the fielder to move towards the ball. The fielder must stand up and catch the tossed ball after it has bounced one time.
Level 2--The tosser stands facing the fielder about 6 feet away from the fielder's head. The fielder must get up and catch the tossed ball before it bounces.
Level 3--The tosser stands about one foot behind the fielder's feet. On "Go!," the tosser tosses the ball **straight up into the air,** and the fielder must stand up and catch the tossed ball after it has bounced once.
Level 4--The tosser stands behind the fielder's feet, and the fielder must stand and catch the tossed ball before it bounces.

Willie Mays

Purpose: To practice advanced tossing, catching, and visual tracking skills.

Supplies: One ball for every 2 students. Have balls of various size available.

Set-Up: Pairs scattered in open space, one student with the ball standing behind their partner.

Procedure:

The student with the ball is the tosser, and the other student is the fielder. The tosser stands behind the fielder, with the fielder facing away from the tosser. The tosser gives two commands to their partner: on "Go," the fielder begins to jog away from the tosser; and, on "Ball," the fielder looks up to visually track the ball that has just been tossed up and over the fielder's head.

The ball must be tossed **up, over, and out in front of** the fielder so that the fielder will be able to move to the ball. The object of this activity is for the fielder to catch the ball "On The Move."

Change positions.

Reverse Willie

Purpose: To practice advanced tossing and catching skills.

Supplies: One ball for every two students. Have various size balls available.

Set-Up: Partners scattered in open space facing each other, one student with the ball.

face tosser

reach behind

Procedure:

The student with the ball is the tosser, and the other student is the fielder. Facing each other, 3-4 feet apart, the tosser tosses the ball high into the air. The fielder lines up the ball with the center of his forehead, takes one step forward and catches the ball behind his back. The fielder's body should remain erect.

Teaching Cue: head up, back straight.

Movement Cards

Movement Cards™ Deck* is a set of 240 individual activity cards divided into twelve distinct suits. Words appear on each card in English, Spanish, French and German. The suits are:

> soccer - futbol - football - fubball
> tennis - tenis - tennis - tennis
> football - futbol America - football Americain - fubball
> grapes - uvas - raisins - wientraube
> apple - manazana - pomme - apfel
> bird - pajaro - oiseau - vogel
> dog - perro - chein - hund
> cat - gato - chat - katze
> diamond - diamante - diamant - raute
> rectangle - retangulo - rectangle - rechteck
> traingle - triangle - trianglo - triangle - dreieck

Each suit is numbered one through twenty. The suits are used to designate an activity. The numbers on the cards are used to indicate the number of repetitions of the activity. The purpose of Movement Cards™ is to move students, identify repetitive numbers and simultaneously teach reading and multi-lingual skills. The teacher has the option of determining activities: i.e., exercise, balance, sports skill development, gymnastic, etc. The activities selected will be determined by their curriculum, and teaching techniques.

*John Thomson, *Movement Cards™ Deck* (Dallas: U.S.Games).

Movement Cards™ Miming

Purpose: To develop communication skills.

Supplies: One Movement Cards™ Deck.

Set-Up: Students scattered in open space.

Procedure:

This is a non-verbal activity. Place Movement Cards face down in a pile. Each student selects one Movement Card. Without showing their card to another person, and without saying a word or making a sound, students find other students that have picked up a card of the same suit by giving **GESTURES** as clues. For example, if a diamond was the suit drawn, a student might point to the ring finger as a clue. Once the students have grouped together by suits, each group lines themselves up from the lowest to highest numbers. Again, students do not talk to each other, they only use gestures.

Movement Cards™ Math

Purpose: To practice mathematic and communication skills.

Supplies: One Movement Cards™ Deck.

Set-Up: Students scattered in open space.

the answer is 32

addition

multiply

addition & subtraction

Procedure:

Place Movement Cards face down in a pile. Each student selects one card. The teacher verbally gives the answer to a math problem and it is the students' task to use their cards to add, subtract, multiply, and/or divide to solve the mathematic problem. Students do not have to use the same suits.

Examples: The answer is 32. Two students could add a 20 and a 12, two other students could multiply a 16 and a 2 or three students could add a 20 and a 20 and subtract an 8 to get the correct answer.

Movement Cards™ and Motor Skills

Purpose: To practice and master motor skills.

Supplies: Movement Cards™ Deck, plastic cone signs, boundary marker cones, and various equipment determined by the motor skill.

Set-Up: Open space.

Procedure:
Stations can be arranged to accommodate:
- various skills within an activity (basketball tasks for shooting, passing, ball handling and dribbling).
- different equipment (tasks with a rhythm lesson could employ ropes, balls, hoops and wands).
- skills with common movement patterns (overhead throw, tennis serve and forward pass).

Examples:
2 of Grapes (*English*)--The Grape suit could be a **lay-up** for Basketball. The student who drew this card would perform 2 lay-ups
5 of Perro (*Spanish*)--The Perro suit could be **jumping jacks**. The student who drew this card would perform 5 jumping jacks.
9 of Pomme (*French*)--The Pomme suit could be a **double under**. The student who drew this card would perform 9 double unders with the jump rope.
20 of Raute (*German*)--The Raute suit could be **setting** a volleyball. The student who draws this card would set a volleyball 20 times.

Rubber Chicken Activities

The ultimate "teaching by distraction" teaching supply. Using the rubber chicken will spice up your traditional games and skill drills. When you don't need an object to bounce, such as a baton, beanbag or deck ring, try using the rubber chicken in place of a standard item. Students will accomplish the same outcomes but with a little twist.

For example, use a rubber chicken as an "it" designator to transform an ordinary game of frozen tag into *Barnyard Tag*. Or substitute a few faux fowls for regular batons and your racers will find themselves competing on the "Rubber Chicken Circuit." Rather than playing popcorn with balls, put a flock of birds on a parachute then challenge the kids to help them "fly the coop."

Have fun with your students using the following ***Rubber Chicken Activities.***

Barnyard Boogie

Purpose: To practice fundamental motor skills, and to develop creativity and cooperation.

Supplies: One rubber chicken for each group of 4-6 students and lively music.

Set-Up: Groups of 4-6 students in a single file line..

Procedure:

This is the modern version of *Tag Along* (see *Camouflage Fitness*). Students move in single file with the leader choosing the path. The first student in line hands a rubber chicken to the next person in line and they hand it to the next student. When the rubber chicken reaches the last student, they jog to the front of the line and continue the hand-off progression. Instead of walking, as in *Tag Along,* the leading student chooses a locomotor movement for the rest of the group to mimic. (The leader may want to add arm movements and different levels to their movement, to the beat of the music.) The group continues to travel and perform the first student's moves until the chicken reaches the end of the line and the last person rotates to the front. The new leader will create a new method of traveling that the group will mimic. Each student is encouraged to create their own movement sequence to the music.

Rotisserie Chicken

Purpose: To develop eye-hand coordination and flexibility, and cooperation

Supplies: One *Rubber Chicken* for every 5-6 students.

Set-Up: Equal groups of 5-6 students in relay lines, scattered in open space.

Procedure:

This is the "chicken" version of *Over and Under*. In groups of 5-6, the first student passes the chicken over her head to the next student who passes the chicken between her legs, and the next over her head. When the chicken reaches the last person in line, she runs to the front of the line and the procedure of over and under starts again. When the person who was at the front of the line works their way back to that position, **the team's chicken is cooked and the entire line sits down.**

Variations:
- See how fast your team can cook the chicken.
- Can you cook your chicken before the music stops?

Chicken Catch-A-Tori

Purpose: To improve chasing and fleeing skills and cardiorespiratory endurance.

Supplies: One rubber chicken for every 4 students.

Set-Up: Students scattered in open space.

Procedure:

This is the "chicken" version of *Touch-and-Go Tag* (see *Bean Bag and Ball Handling* section). Begin the activity with at least one fourth of the students holding a rubber chicken. The student with the rubber chicken is the designated "it." When another student is touched by "it" they gain possession of the chicken and become the new tagger. **Taggers tag with their free hand, not the chicken.** Taggers cannot tag another "it." They can have only one chicken at a time.

Variations:

● After a student is tagged they must run through the chicken coop. (Devise a tunnel with mats or an obstacle marked-off with cones.)

Barnyard Tag

Purpose: To develop chasing and fleeing skills.

Supplies: Scrimmage vest for one-fourth of the class and rubber chickens for one-fourth of the class.

Set-Up: Students scattered in open space.

Procedure:

This is a modern version of frozen tag. One-fourth of the students wear scrimmage vests designating them as "it" (Chicken Hawks). Another one-fourth of the students each carry a chicken (Superchickens). The rest of the class are regular chickens.

When the game starts, chickens scatter and the Chicken Hawks try to **tag** the regular chickens. If tagged, a chicken is "frozen." The Superchickens go around the barnyard (playing area) reviving the "frozen" chickens by giving them a chicken. The unfrozen chicken now becomes a Superchicken. The old Super-chicken now becomes a regular chicken.

Frequent Flyers

Purpose: To develop muscular strength and cooperation.

Supplies: One mini parachute (6') and one rubber chickens for every 6-8 students.

Set-Up: Groups of 6-8 students around a mini parachute scattered in open space.

Procedure:

This is a modern version of *Parachute Popcorn*. Instead of placing a number of balls in the middle of the parachute, use a chicken and watch it *fly* up and down. Count how *frequently* students can toss the chicken up and down on the parachute in a set amount of time.

Variations:

• See how high each group can toss the chicken before it flies away (goes off the chute).

• Use more than one chicken.

Hot Wings

Purpose: To develop spatial awareness and directionality, eye-hand
coordination and cooperation

Supplies: One Miniparachute (6') for each 6-8 students, and one rubber
chicken for each pair of parachute groups.

Set-Up: Two groups of 6-8 students adjacent to each other scattered in
open space.

Procedure:

Two groups work together flipping a rubber chicken back and forth to each
other's miniparachute. A point is scored for **both** groups each time a rubber
chicken is successfully caught in a miniparachute. See how many points your
groups can make in a set time limit.

Pair-up with another group and continue.

Variation:

- *Double Order of Hot Wings*--Each group flips a rubber chicken at the same
time.
- *Foul Ball*--A stationary group flips the chicken to a group with the parachute
"on the move."

Chicken and Dumplings

Purpose: To develop spatial awareness and directionality, eye-hand coordination and cooperation.

Supplies: One mini parachute (6'), two beanbags, one Gator Skin® Softi ball, one hula hoop and one rubber chicken per group of 6-8 students.

Set-Up: Groups scattered in open space with their supplies.

Procedure:

Using a mixing bowl (mini parachute), vegetables (two bean bags), one dumpling (Gator Skin® Softi ball), a kettle (hula hoop), and one chicken (the rubber chicken), the chefs (students) must cook their meal: *Chicken and Dumplings.* The Assistant Chef (the hoop holder), stands away from the mixing bowl and holds the kettle out in front of his body. The Head Chef stands next to the Assistant Chef prepared to catch the ingredients. The Apprentice Chefs (parachute holders), flip the ingredients--one at a time--from the mixing bowl **into the kettle** to be caught by the Head Chief.

If an ingredient does not go through the kettle or goes through but is dropped by the Head Chef, it goes back to the mixing bowl to be prepared again, (flipped from the parachute). Once all the ingredients have been properly prepared the students rotate positions and assume a new role.

Always Remember:

Inch by Inch
It's a Cinch

Yard by Yard
It's too Hard

Rubber Bass
Activities

"Gone Fishing," is a sign you may see, or a least, used to see on a store front when the owner wanted to go "have some fun," during the work day. Your students will also have fun and be successful using a Rubber Bass as a manipulative: turning old activities into new fishing stories. The saying, *"you should have seen the one that got away,"* will definitely take on a new meaning.

Have fun and enjoy these activities with your students.

Flying Fish

Purpose: To develop throwing and catching skills.

Supplies: One Poly Spot™ or small boundary cone for every student, and one Rubber Bass for each pair.

Set-Up: Pairs facing each other, scattered, with enough room to move backwards into open space.

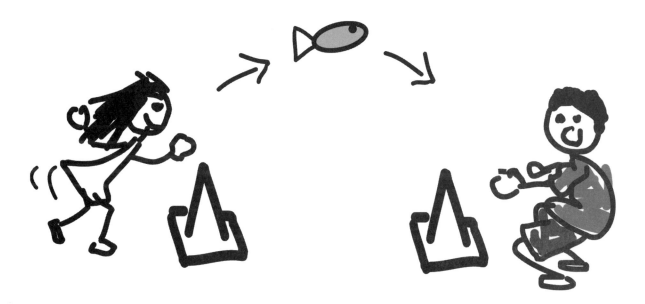

Procedure:

Partners stand 2 giant steps apart from each other with a poly spot or cone directly in front of them as a location marker. The purpose is to successfully throw and catch a rubber bass to each other staying behind their marker. Each time the catcher successfully catches the rubber bass, the **catcher** moves their marker back one step. If the thrown object is dropped or caught in front of the marker, the marker is moved toward the thrower one step. **Only the catcher's mark is moved.**

Continue throwing and catching to see how far apart partners can get during a set time limit.

Fishing Hole

Purpose: To improve throwing and tossing skills, agility, cardiorespiratory endurance, and cooperation.

Supplies: One hula hoop, one Poly Spot™ and one Rubber Bass for every 3 students.

Set-Up: Groups of 3 students scattered in open space.

Procedure:

Begin with the poly spot and hoop at least 2 giant steps apart, moving objects farther apart as skill progresses. The poly spot is designated the "fishing pier" with the tosser standing on it. The hoop is the "pond" with the retriever standing behind it facing the pier. The third person, the observer, stands in line behind the tosser. The pond has been over fished and needs to be restocked by these Conservation Officers. The tosser tries to toss the Rubber Bass into the fishing hole (hula hoop) from the pier (poly spot). If he is successful this group scores a point for the environment. (The fish must be completely inside the hoop.) The tosser then runs behind the pond taking the place of the retriever. The retriever picks up the Rubber Bass, runs to the pier and **PLACES** it on the poly spot, and then stands in line behind the pier and becomes the observer. The observer now becomes the tosser.

Repeat the sequence.

Catch and Release

Purpose: To develop catching and throwing skills.

Supplies: One hoop and one rubber bass for every 3 students.

Set-Up: Three students in a line prepared to move forward in an open space.

Procedure:
Three students are in a line (a tosser, a hoop holder, and a catcher). The tosser faces the catcher with the hoop holder in the middle. The tosser tosses the *Rubber Bass* through the hoop to the catcher. After catching the Fish the catcher pivots half way around facing forward and becomes the tosser, the hoop holder moves in front of the new tosser and the old tosser becomes the catcher. The object of this activity is to move, in groups of three, from one boundary line forward to another boundary line while *Catching and Releasing the Rubber Bass.*

Variations:
- The catcher uses a net ball bag to catch the Rubber Bass. Name the activity *Bag the Bass.*

Fish Monger

Purpose: To develop eye-hand coordination, catching skills, muscular endurance and cooperation.

Supplies: One mini parachute (6') and one Rubber Bass for each group of 6-8 students.

Set-Up: Groups of 6-8 students around a mini parachute with one person standing away from the parachute.

Procedure:

Using a scale (mini parachute) to weigh the fish (rubber bass) the Fish Mongers (parachute holders) flip the fish to a customer (student) who is standing away from the scale). The customer catches the fish and decides tthat he is not hungry. He takes the fish back to the scale. A new customer moves away from the scale and the Fish Mongers flip the fish again.

Continue rotating positions. In a set amount of time, see how many different customers can the Fish Mongers successfully flip the fish to.

Fish Stew

Purpose: To develop spatial awareness and directionality, eye-hand coordination and cooperation.

Supplies: One mini parachute (6'), 2 beanbags, one Gator Skin® Softi ball, one hula hoop and one rubber bass per group of 6-8 students.

Set-Up: Groups scattered in open space with their supplies.

Procedure:

Using a mixing bowl (mini parachute), vegetables (two bean bags), one potato (Gator Skin® Softi ball), a kettle (hula hoop), and one fish (the rubber bass), the chefs (students) must cook their meal: F*ish Stew*. The Assistant Chef (the hoop holder), stands away from the mixing bowl and holds the kettle out in front of her body. The Head Chef stands next to the Assistant Chef prepared to catch the ingredients. The Apprentice Chefs (parachute holders), flip the ingredients--one at a time--from the mixing bowl **into the kettle** to be caught by the Head Chief.

If an ingredient does not go through the kettle or goes through but is dropped by the Head Chef, it goes back to the mixing bowl to be prepared again, (flipped from the parachute). Once all the ingredients have been properly prepared the students rotate positions and assume a new role.

Don't wait for your ship to come in.

Row out to meet it.

Spots
and
Cones

Boundaries are a part of every lesson and every teaching strategy. They bring order to lessons, and assist in student management. They set limits. Students move to or from a place. Groups are designated by specific colors and numbers. Border lines and various shapes define restricted areas and determine success. For example, consider *boundary* words in a game of basketball: endline, backcourt, out of bounds, and key.

Spots and cones are an easy, inexpensive way to teach boundaries. They are an indispensable teaching supply in every class. Students may work in small groups and use flexible boundaries, setting their own limits as needed for success. Use spots and cones to teach sequencing, number and color recognition along with motor skills to enhance classroom management.

Both spots and cones are available in many different sizes and colors. The spots are flat markers, made of soft flexible plastic from 2" to 24" in diameter. The cones are plastic with weighted bases, 6" to 36" tall.

On Your Mark

Purpose: To develop spatial awareness fundamental movement skills.

Supplies: One 9" Poly Spot™ for each student.

Set-Up: Students scattered, standing on their poly spots.

Procedure:
Students perform the following tasks in relationship to their spot:
- How many times can you foot run around your spot in 15 seconds? Use other locomotor movements. Reverse directions.
- Jump over your spot. How high can you jump over your spot? How many times can you clap your hands as you jump over your spot? Turn in the air as you jump over your spot.
- Move in a variety of directions in relationship to the spot in addition to jumping over it, such as: to the side, onto, out of, in front of, in the back of.
- Balance on your spot. Balance with one body parts on your spot. Balance with different body parts on your spot. How many different body parts can you balance on?

Jumping Beans

Purpose: To improve agility, flexibility, directionality, cardiorespiratory, endurance and coordinatition

Supplies: Four 9" Poly Spots™ and 2 bean bags for every 3 students.

Set-Up: Groups of 3 students in relay pattern approximately 20-30 feet apart.

Procedure:

Four poly spots are spaced at even intervals between the two boundary lines. Two students stand in line at one end of the pathway and one student stands at the other end. A bean bag is placed on the first and third poly spot. When the music begins, the first student in the line of two students runs to the first poly spot, picks up the beanbag, runs to the second poly spot and places it on the empty spot, runs to the third spot and picks up the beanbag and places it on the fourth spot. She then tags the person standing at the end of the pathway who reverses the sequence. See how many times the group can complete the sequence during a set amount of time.

Variations:

- Have each student wear a Polar Edge™ Heart Rate Monitor maintaining the sequence until her beeper alarm sounds. The runner would run around the end student rather than tag them to continue the sequence.

Round Up

Purpose: To improve eye-foot coordination and cardiorespiratory endurance.

Supplies: One ball for each student (basketball, volleyball, soccer or play - ground ball), and at least one cone for each student.

Set-Up: Cones placed throughout the activity area, students scattered among the cones.

Procedure:

When the music starts, students foot dribble around the cones. Students must dribble completely around the cone before moving to the next cone. The challenge is to see how many different cones they can dribble around in a set amount of time.

Variations:

- Alternate between hand and foot dribbling.
- Number the cones. Have students begin the activity in a "shot gun" rotation and dribble around numbered cones consecutively.
- Students work in pairs passing the ball to each other "X" number of times before going around the next cone.

Round Up and Stop

Purpose: To improve eye-foot coordination and cardiorespiratory endurance.

Supplies: One 9" poly spot, one cone and one ball for each student (basketball, volleyball, soccer or playground ball).

Set-Up: Cones and spots placed throughout the activity area. Students

Procedure:

When the music starts, students dribble around the cones. The challenge is to see how many different cones they can dribble around **and** how many different spots they can stop the ball on. Students alternate dribbling around a cone then stopping on a spot. After stopping on a spot, if the students are hand-dribbling they are to begin dribbling again with the other hand. If they are foot-dribbling, they foot-trap the ball on the poly spot, then dribble to the next cone.

Students see many different cones they can go around and how many different spots can they stop on. Challenge students to set their own World Records while maintaining control of their ball.

Rainbow Round Up and Stop

Purpose: To develop coordination, cardiorespiratory endurance and color recognition.

Supplies: One ball, (basketball, volleyball, soccer or play ground ball),), one 9" poly Spot™ and one cone for each student--use the 8 color set of spots and cones.

Set-Up: Colored cones and spots placed throughout the activity area. Students stand on a spot with a ball.

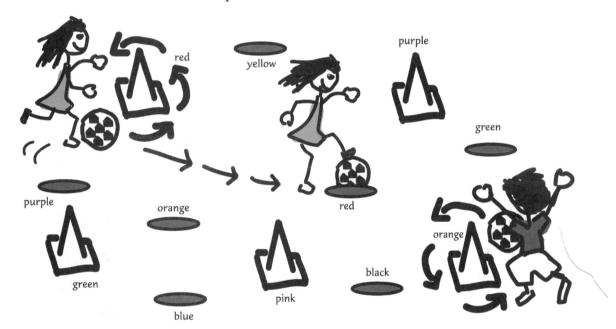

Procedure:

This activity is the same format as *Round Up and Stop* with color recognition added.

When the music starts, students dribble around the cones. The challenge is to see how many different colored cones they can dribble around **and** how many different spots they can stop the ball on. Students alternate dribbling around a cone then stopping on a spot. If they dribble around a red cone, they must stop on a red poly spot. **A different color must be selected after each successful stop.**

After stopping a spot, if the students are hand-dribbling they are to begin dribbling again with the other hand. If they are foot-dribbling they foot trap the ball on the poly spot then dribble to the next cone.

Mutant Hop Scotch

Purpose: To improve agility, sequencing, cardiorespiratory endurance and cooperation.

Supplies: Five 9" Poly Spots™ for every group of 3 students.

Set-Up: Groups of 3 students scattered, with a set of 5 spots. Place the spots in a grid formation (rectangle with one spot in the center).

1. UP & BACK

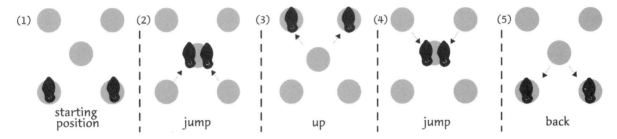

2. BOTH FEET

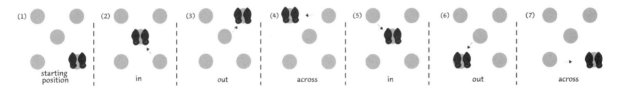

3. TURN AROUND

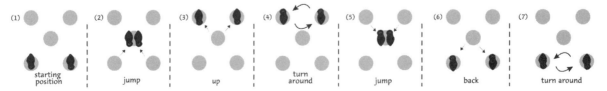

(continued on the next page)

Procedure:
The size of the grid is determined by the age and ability of the students. The grid should not exceed 2' x 3' in size. Students should become familiar with one sequence on the grid before adding another.

In each group of 3 students there is a jumper, a counter, and an observer. The jumper performs the jumping sequence.The counter counts the number of complete sequences performed by the jumper. The observer counts the number of spots missed. Accuracy is just as important as quickness.

Students perform the following challenges:
How many *Up and Backs* can you accurately perform in a set amount of time?
How many *Both Feet* can you accurately perform in a set amount of time?
How many *Turn Arounds* can you accurately perform in a set amount of time?

After students have **mastered** each of the 3 sequences, combine the sequences for an even greater challenge. A sample combined sequence could be: 5 *Up and Backs*, 5 *Both Feet* and 5 *Turn Arounds*.

Encourage students to set PR's (Personal Records) for time.

"Seven days without exercise makes one weak."

Rudy Benton

Cooperatives

Even though our society honors competitiveness and a single winner of an event, most of our success is the result of cooperating with others. Students who develop skills for being responsible members of a group increase their chances for success. Successful groups are composed of both leaders and nonleaders who cooperate to achieve a goal. As students participate in *COOPERATIVE ACTIVITIES* in Physical Education they can transfer this knowledge and ability to any aspect of their lives, and can begin using the skills to enhance communication and overall effectiveness of relationships.

In focusing on activities that specifically promote cooperation, allow students time at the beginning of the activity to discuss ways they will solve the problem; and time at the end to reflect on the specific components used to successfully perform the task. Some of these components may include: communicating, cooperating, encouraging, listening, being kind, patient and understanding.

Up and At 'Em

Purpose: To develop agility, cooperation, and upper body strength.

Supplies: One ball for every 2 students.

Set-Up: Pairs scattered in open space.

Procedure:

From a standing position, partners hold a ball between their foreheads. The challenge is to lower their bodies to a push-up position without touching the ball with their hands or dropping it. If successful in getting down, they then try to get back up onto their feet. How many times can students go all the way to the floor and back *Up And At 'Em?*

Variations:
- Perform this challenge without talking to each other.
- Discuss with each other the cooperative process.
- Form a group of three for this task.

Partner Ball Carries

Purpose: To develop agility, spatial awareness and cooperation.

Supplies: One ball for every 2 students.

Set-Up: Pairs scattered in open space.

Procedure:
Partners carry a ball between their bodies through a designated course or to a designated spot without touching each other or the ball with their hands.

Variations:
- Use different size balls.
- Set up high, medium, and low levels in the designated course.
- Determine your best time.
- Blindfold one partner and let their partner talk them through the course.

Group Ball Carries

Purpose: To develop agility, spatial awareness and cooperation.

Supplies: Four balls for every 5 students.

Set-Up: Group of 5 students scattered in open space.

Procedure:

Groups of five students carry four balls from a designated spot to a designated spot. The procedure is the same as *Partner Ball Carries.* A ball has to be carried between the students' bodies. The students cannot touch each other nor can a ball be touched by a hand.

Variations:

- Bodies are at different levels.
- Balls are placed at different levels.
- Students form smaller or larger groups. Always have one less ball than the number of students.

Amoeba

Purpose: To use fundamental motor skills and movement concepts in groups.

Supplies: One Chinese jump rope for every 4-6 students, music.

Set-Up: Groups of 4-6 students inside a rope, groups scattered.

Procedure:

Groups of 4-6 students are inside a Chinese jump rope. When the music starts, the teacher announces a specific locomotor movement (skip, gallop, hop, slid). The Amoebas travel around the activity space performing the movement. When the music stops, the groups stop and the teacher announces a shape e.g., square, circle, oval, heart, star, numbers, letters. The Amoebas form the shape.

Variations:

- Use a combination of student designed locomotor movements, e.g., walk 8, slide 8, jump 8, repeat, to move the rope.
- Use music that corresponds to fast/slow and light/heavy movements.
- Perform the locomotor movement and/or the shape at different levels.

Amoeba Shapes

Purpose: To use spacial awareness, problem solving and cooperation.

Supplies: One Chinese jump rope for every 4-6 students.

Set-Up: Groups of 4-6 students inside a rope, groups scattered.

shape
idaho

letter
first letter of
capital of idaho

number
13-9

Procedure:
Groups of 4-6 students are inside a Chinese jump rope. Various questions are posed to the groups. They must respond to the question by forming the correct shape with their group. Examples of questions: form the shape of the state that is famous for Sun Valley and potatoes, form the first letter of the capital of Idaho, the number of days in a week, 42 divided by 6. The questions are endless.

Variations:
- Students submit questions for the group to answer.
- Classroom teachers contribute to the questions based on classroom curricula.
- Use questions from The Trivial Pursuit game.

Drills to Thrill
not
Drills to kill.

Specialty Activities

The Forest

Purpose: To improve fitness and fundamental motor skill development. This activity may be adapted to almost any unit in reviewing specific motor skills and also may be used in conjunction with a science unit on ecology.

Supplies: At least one bowling pin per student, and other available supplies, e.g., dome markers, hoops, ropes, Spider Balls™, rubber chicken and rubber bass.

Set-Up: Place items randomly throughout the activity area. Space items far enough apart to allow a pathway and close enough to present obstacles.

tree

spider   stump   pond

Procedure:

To create *The Forest* scenario, let the following supplies represent various parts of a forest: trees--bowling pins, stumps--dome markers, ponds--hula hoops,

(continued on the next page)

snakes--ropes, spider--spider balls™, wild chickens--rubber chickens, fish-out-of-the-water--rubber bass.

Traveling through The Forest
When the music starts, students begin their journey through *The Forest*. They travel through the forest without touching any objects, without jumping over any objects, and without touching any other travelers. Perform various locomotor movement forward and backward, fast and slow and at different levels.

Students may create a Big Book describing their forest. Encourage imagination.

Cutting and Planting Trees in The Forest
As trees are cut down by the lumberjacks to be used for paper, to build houses, etc., new trees must be planted. When the music starts students are allowed to "cut" down trees. A tree is considered "chopped down" when a student knocks over a bowling pin using a **knee, elbow, chin or hip.** In order to "save the forest" students must replant (stand-up) a pin. Now as students move throughout The Forest, before they chop down a second tree, they must replant a tree (stand up a bowling pin). Repeat until music stops. How many trees can be chopped down and new ones planted in a set amount of time?

Variation:
- The lumberjack must throw a beanbag and knock over the tree (bowling pin).
- The lumberjack hikes (bends over and toss between legs) a bean bag and chops down the trees.

Partners in The Forest
One person is designated the "Planter," the other person is the "Lumberjack." The Lumberjack "cuts" down the trees by knocking down the pin with their knee, elbow, chin or hip. The Planter quickly follows behind their partner to "plant" trees, by standing up the pin.

Sports Related Uses for The Forest Scenario.
Basketball--Everyone has a basketball and dribbles through the forest working on dribbling skills and ball handling skills.

Soccer--Everyone works on soccer dribbling skills by dribbling through the forest. Soccer dribbling skills are best performed using a spider ball.

Chinese Jump Rope

Purpose: To improve rhythmical jumping, leg strength and endurance, cardio-respiratory endurance, coordination, balance and cooperation. This is a great activity for use in a study of China.

Supplies: One Chinese jump rope for every 3 students.

Set-Up: Groups of 3 students scattered in open space with one rope.

starting position   in position

out position   on position

Procedure:

Two students are holding the rope around their ankles and one student stands between the holders ready to jump. The rope holders should have their feet shoulder-width apart.

Following is the basic sequence. The jumper begins with one foot inside the rope and the other foot outside the rope, then jumps sideways so that the foot that was inside the rope goes out, and the foot that was outside goes in, and then back to the starting position. The sequence is four sideways straddle, (straddle--straddle--straddle--straddle).

Next the jumper jumps with both feet *inside* the rope (in), then both feet *outside* the rope (out), then *in* again and last, both feet *on* the rope (right foot on right rope and left foot on left rope.)

The complete sequence is:
straddle--straddle--straddle--straddle
in--out--in--on

Each time the jumper successfully completes the sequence, the rope is raised a couple of inches and the jumper performs the sequence at the new height. When a jumper misses, they stay at the same level until they are successful. See how many different levels a jumper can successfully jump in a set amount of time. The jumper starts at the lowest level each time.

Variations:
- The jumper turns in the opposite direction after each straddle.
- Add a criss-cross, e.g., in--out--criss-cross--on.

Scooter Triathlon

Purpose: To develop cardiorespiratory, arm and leg strength and endurance, and agility.

Supplies: One scooter board with handles for every 2 students.

Set-Up: Partners, in a line, on the side line of the activity area.

swim

run

bike

Procedure:

This activity simulates an official Triathlon: swim, bike and run. It is a timed partner event--how many times can they perform the event within a set time limit.

Students travel to a turning around point/marker and back to their partner. Both students perform each segment of the Triathlon before they start on the next portion of the event. To "swim," students lay on their stomach on the scooter board and push forward with their hands and feet. To "bike," they sit on the scooter board, facing forward, holding the handles and they *pedal* forward going around the marker and back to their partner. To "run," they lean forward from a standing position, feet in back of the scooter, hands on the scooter handle, with weight on the scooter and run forward pushing the scooter.

Kup™ Stax*

Purpose: To improve eye hand coordination, agility, laterality, sequencing, and cooperation.

Supplies: One set of Kup™ Stack cups for every 3-4 students. (These cups are specifically designed for this activity. Other cups may splinter and cause injury.)

Set-Up: Students around a table or other smooth flat surface, approximately waist high.

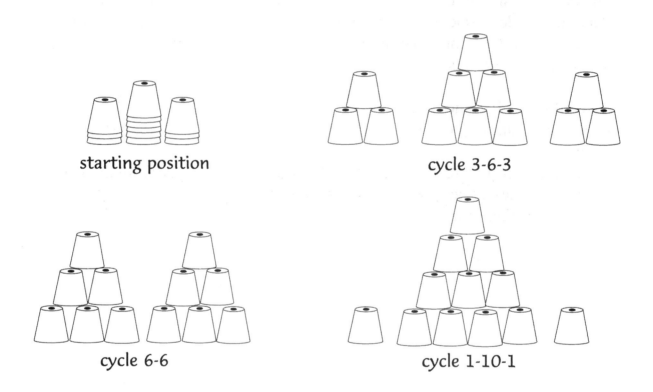

starting position

cycle 3-6-3

cycle 6-6

cycle 1-10-1

Procedure:

The object of this activity is to stack and unstack 12 plastic cups as fast as you can into 3 pyramids. Students compete against themselves setting their own "World Record," or compete as a team challenging other school teams.

*Adapted from: *Kup™Stax* (Pawtucket: Hasbro Publishers, 1995).

(continues on the next page)

A student begins with his hands flat on the playing surface with 3 stacks of cups in front of him in the following order--one stack of 3 cups, one stack of 6 cups, and one stack of 3 cups. Each stack is about one foot from the other. On the signal "Go!" the cupstacker begins by "upstacking" the cups: form a pyramid with the first set of 3 cups, then a pyramid of 6 cups, and then a pyramid of three cups. Next, the cupstacker "downstacks" the cups: first by returning to the first 3-cup pyramid and converting each pyramid back to the original stack of cups. At the conclusion of the sequence, the cups are in the 3-6-3 downstack combination.

Once students have mastered the 3-6-3 combination they are ready for the Kup™Stax cycle. The cycle is used in tournaments and intramural programs. The cycle consists of upstacking and downstacking the 3-6-3 combination, up-stacking and downstacking the 6-6 combination, and upstacking and down-stacking the 1-10-1 combination. At the conclusion of the cycle the cups are in the downstack 3-6-3 combination.

Helpful Hints for Success:
- Begin by stacking one cup at a time using one hand. This is the 1-1-1 method.
- Next master the 2-2-2 method. Use 2 hands and take 2 cups from the stack and practice upstacking and down stacking.
- View the *Kup™Stax* video.

Kin® Ball*
Physical Education Version

Purpose: To develop striking skills and reaction time in a cooperative team game.

Supplies: One **Omnikin Ball**® (4' ball recommended) and scrimmage vests: a different colored set of vests for each team. Four players on a team with the maximum number of 8 teams/colors.

Set-Up: Large playing area.

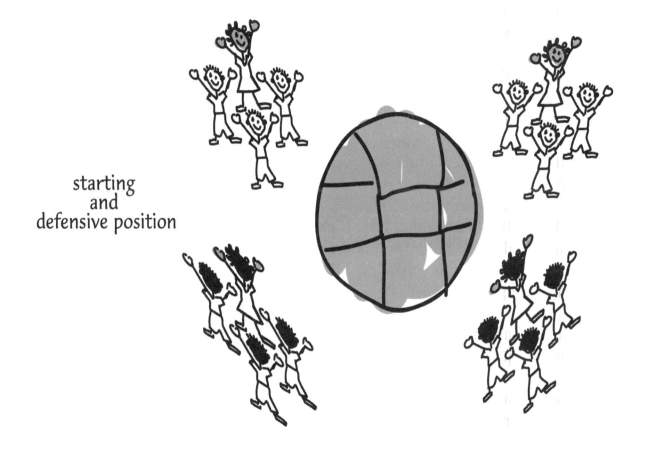

starting
and
defensive position

*Adapted from: Mario,Demers, *Official Rules for the Kin®Ball Activity* (Sharny, Qc., Canada: Omnikin Inc., 1995).

Procedure:
Each team begins with zero points. The goal is to end the game with **zero** points.

striker

Players are divided into 4-8 teams depending on the class size, with four players on a team. The name of each team is the color of their scrimmage vest.

Before play begins, each team must decide the striking (hitting or serving) order of players. This order must remain the same throughout the game--it does **not** change. Each player is responsible for a specific area. The basic defensive formation is for the players to form a square around the ball.

The team that starts the game,"Tees Up" the ball for their striker.It is mandatory for ALL holders to have one knee touching the ground and both hands in contact with the ball before the ball is served by the striker. When the striking team's holders and their striker is ready, the striker calls out "Omnikin." The Physical Education teacher, then calls out a team color just **before** the Striker hits the ball. The ball must travel at least 6' outward. The team whose color is called must rush to the ball before it hits the ground and "Tee-It-Up" for their Striker to hit the ball. Team members may use any part of their bodies to keep the ball from touching the ground.

The Physical Education Teacher calls out the different colors in an unpredictable rotation as quickly as possible to maintain continuous action.

Because of the nonstop action of this game, playing time can be divided into quarters or halves for resting purposes.

(continued on the next page)

Teams **do not** want to score points. A team **receives one point** when a foul (mistake) is committed.

Fouls:

- Allowing the ball to hit the ground when your team color is called.
- Hitting the ball out of bounds.
- Interfering on purpose with another team's access to the ball.
- Contacting the ball by the striker before all holders have both hands in contact with the ball.
- Failure of a holder to have a least one knee on the ground before the ball is struck.
- Striker hitting the ball with one hand (contact must be made with two hands.)
- Striker failing to hit the ball so it travels at least 6' parallel to the ground.
- A striker hitting the ball out of striking sequence.
- A striker hitting the ball before the teacher calls the color.

For detailed instruction view the *Kin® Ball Instructional Video.*

Mass Soccer

Purpose: To practice soccer skills. Students must have developed basic soccer skills of dribbling and passing, goal tending, and tackling, and have an understanding of offensive and defensive strategies.

Supplies: For each group of 8 students: 8 scrimmage vests, 2 cones, 7 bean bags and one Gator Skin® Softi ball ALL THE SAME COLOR, plus one small hoop.

Set-Up: Teams of 8 students set up their own goals in a **large** circle formation. Each goal is comprised of 2 cones (same color) placed 6'-8' apart. At the right side of the goal is a ring. At the left side of the goal place the 7 bean bags (all the same color.) *See illustration of set-up on the back of this page.*

Procedure:

All players on the same team must wear the same color scrimmage vest. Each group decides the number of offensive and defensive players ensuring everyone has a position. **All teams must have a Goal Keeper.**

A kickoff is started in the middle of the circle area with one offensive player from each team with their team ball, (maximum of 8 teams, 8 different color balls) No other players may be in the kickoff area. **The object of the game is to be the first team to score one goal on each of the other seven teams.**

When a goal is scored, the **Scorer** (not a Goalie or any other team member) retrieves the ball for her teammates to continue playing. Upon completing a goal, the **Scorer** gets to take a bean bag away from the team she just scored against. The Scorer then places the colored bean bag in the hoop to the right of *their* goal. Example:

> If the blue team scored a goal on the purple team, the Scorer for the blue team retrieves the ball and passes it back to his team. He then takes a purple beanbag.back to his goal and places it in the hoop.

After all seven goals have been scored, and all seven different colored bean bags have been placed in the hoop, all members of the team go back to their goal and sit down.

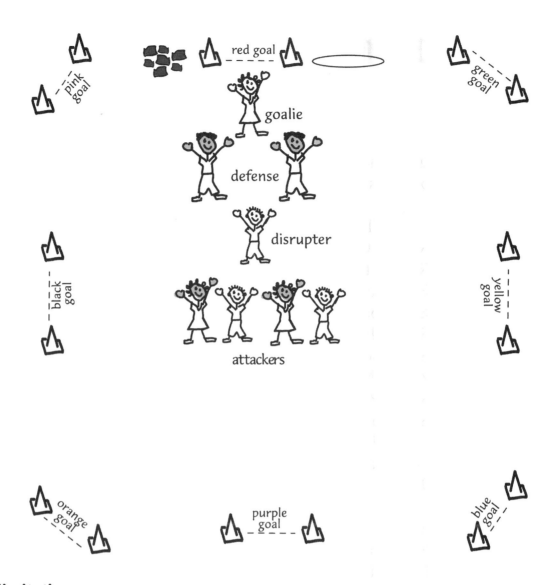

Game limitations:

- Bean bags are not to be thrown at any time. They must be carried and placed in the hoop. If a student throws it, their team loses that bean bag and must return it.
- If a team ends up with two bean bags of the same color in their ring during any time of the game (means they scored on the same team twice) then ALL of their "point" bean bags will be taken away and given back to the appropriate team. They continue playing; they just start all over.
- Goalies may not kick a ball after saving a goal. They must either roll or underhand throw the ball. (You may want the goalie to use the two hand regulation throw-in.) For any goalie penalty the game is stopped and all bean bags returned to begin the game again.

Recommended Physical Education Supplies

The following supplies are recommended for implementing the teaching strategies in this book, based on a class of 32 students.

4	Cone-Clip-On Message Signs
10	Rubber Chickens
10	Rubber Bass
10	Hula Hoops
8	Basketballs
8	Soccer balls
8	Super Soft Footballs
16	Z-Ball™ balls
16	8 1/2" Playground Balls (2 each of 8 colors)
16	Scrimmage Vests (2 each of 8 colors)
16	Foxtail™ Softies
32	Bean Bags (4 each of 8 colors)
32	9" Poly Spots™ (4 each of 8 colors)
8	Gatorskin® Softi Balls (one of each color)
8	6" Poly Cones (one of each color)
1 set	Rounded Markers, (40 to a set)
8	Deck Rings (one of each color)
4	6' Parachutes
12	Fleece Balls
12	Foam Discs
12	Flying Disc
1	4' Kin-Ball®
8 sets	Kup™Stax Cups
32	Bowling Pins
8	Chinese Jump Ropes
1	Tape/CD Player with Wireless Remote On/Off Switch

Sign Language Numbers

One, 1

Two, 2

Three, 3

Four, 4

Five, 5

Six, 6

Seven, 7

Eight, 8

Nine, 9

Ten, 10

REFERENCES

Books:

Demers, Mario. *Official Rules for the Kin® Ball Activity,* Charny, Canada: Omnikin Inc., 1995.

Editors of Klutz Press and Gallaghan, Mike. *The Official Foxtail Book*, Palo Alto: Klutz Press, 1991.

Graham, George. *Teaching Children Physical Education Becoming A Master Teacher*, Champaign: Human Kinetics Publishers, Inc. 1992.

Hopple, Christine J. *Teaching For Outcomes In Elementary Physical Education*, Champaign: Human Kinetics, Publishers, Inc., 1995.

Katherine, Anne. *Boundries Where You End and I Begin*, New York: Simon & Schuster, 1991.

Kup™Stax, Pawtucket: Hasbro Publishers, 1995.

National Association for Sport and Physical Education, *Moving Into The Future National Physical Education Standards: A Guide to Content and Assessment,* St. Louis: Mosby Year Book, Inc., 1995.

Thomson, John. *Movement Cards™ Deck,* Carrollton, TX.: U.S.Games.

Transformations: Kentucky's Curriculum Framework, Volume I, Frankfort: Kentucky Department of Education, 1993.

Videos

Aime, Mel, *Chineese Jump Rope,* color, 28minutes.

Kup™Stax Instructional Video, Distributed by U.S. Games, Carrollton, TX.

Kin®Ball, Charny, Canada: Omnikin, Inc., 1997.

Audiotape

Joel, Billy. "All Shook Up," *Honeymoon In Vegas*, New York: Sony Music Entertainment Inc., 1992.